Step into a world where the gavels are lighter and the aprons are less stiff. This isn't your average Masonic tome fill
wisdom and ancie
sacred collection c
guaranteed to mak
Worshipful Master (

Whether you're a seasoned brother of the Craft, a curious newcomer, or someone just looking to peek behind the Masonic curtain, this jokebook is your secret handshake into a world of laughter, camaraderie, and good old-fashioned fun. From the quirks of lodge life to the mystical mishaps of Masonic rituals, we've left no stone unturned (and no sacred goat unteased) in our quest to bring a chuckle to your solemn assemblies.

Forget the solemn oaths and serious symbols for a moment; The Lighter Side of the Lodge invites you to view Freemasonry through a different lens – one that magnifies the joy, the brotherhood, and yes, the occasional absurdity of it all.

So, don your aprons, adjust your jewels, and prepare to embark on a journey through the lighter side of Freemasonry. Trust us, you've never seen the Craft quite like this before – it's the one Masonic secret you'll be delighted to share!

Welcome! Remember, in Freemasonry, we square our actions and compass our desires. Except for pizza. Always circle your desires around pizza.

You know, we have a secret handshake. It's so secret, even we forget it sometimes!

Entering Freemasonry is like getting a new set of tools without an instruction manual. Good luck figuring out which end of the gavel is up!
"

"

Don't worry, the only thing we're plotting is how to escape the next committee meeting early.

"

Just think, as a Freemason, you'll be part of a centuries-old tradition of asking, 'Is this meeting almost over?'

Remember, in Freemasonry, every man is your brother. Which means you're about to gain a lot of siblings who borrow money and never return it.

Freemasonry: where you'll learn the art of speaking in symbols, and more importantly, the art of sleeping with your eyes open during lectures.

"

The good news is, as a Freemason, you'll learn to navigate life with morality and ethics. The bad news? You still won't find your way out of IKEA faster.

> Welcome to Freemasonry, where every man is a pillar of strength. And every pillar occasionally needs propping up after a long festive board.

Our rituals are ancient and mysterious. Just like the stains on our lodge carpet.

Joining Freemasonry is a commitment to self-improvement, brotherhood, and... figuring out how to fold your apron properly.

Ever wanted to feel like Indiana Jones? Freemasonry's got ancient artefacts, history, and yes, even some dusty old relics.

"

Freemasonry teaches us to be better men. And occasionally, better actors during our rituals.

Welcome to the brotherhood! Just remember, the only thing we take seriously is our whisky.

In Freemasonry, we're all about building. That includes character, community, and sometimes, a reasonable excuse to miss the meeting.

Remember, a Freemason always conducts himself with dignity and grace. Except during the lodge's annual Christmas Party.

Freemasonry: where you'll find the keys to moral and spiritual enlightenment. Just don't ask us about the keys to the lodge; we lost those last week.

You're about to learn the ancient secrets of Masonry. First lesson: never reveal the WiFi password.

In the lodge, you'll find brotherhood, wisdom, and, occasionally, someone's lost jewels.

Becoming a Freemason means you're part of a global fraternity. It also means you're now officially terrible at keeping mundane secrets.

Freemasonry: The only place where you can say you're going to a 'ritual' and it's not weird.

Remember, as a Freemason, every problem is an opportunity in disguise. Like finding out the festive board is vegan.

You'll learn that Masonic rituals are full of symbolism and meaning.
And that 'symbolism and meaning' is code for 'memorising a lot of lines.'

In Freemasonry, we believe in the eternal quest for knowledge. And the eternal question of 'Where did I put my apron?'

Welcome! Just know that the only thing tighter than our brotherhood is our lodge's budget.

As a new candidate, you'll be faced with challenges, trials, and the ultimate test: how to deal with the lodge goat.

You're entering a noble path followed by kings, philosophers, and that guy who can't stop quoting Monty Python.

Our lodge is a place of respect, dignity, and occasionally, epic battles over thermostat settings.

In this brotherhood, you'll learn the value of silence. Especially when you forget your part during the ritual.

Masonry teaches us to be upright in our actions. Except when leaning back in our chairs during a particularly long speech.

Joining Freemasonry is like joining a gym. Except the only weight you'll lift is the weight of moral and ethical responsibility.

In the lodge, we strive for harmony. And that usually means agreeing on which pub to go to after Lodge of Instruction.

You'll learn many things in Freemasonry. For example, 'esoteric' really means 'confusing enough to sound impressive.'

Remember, as a Freemason, your duty is to your God, your country, and finding a polite way to dodge the lodge treasurer's calls.

In Freemasonry, we're all
equals. Which means
everyone equally complains
about the festive board.

The great thing about Freemasonry is its timeless wisdom. And its timelessly confusing bylaws.

In the lodge, we use tools as symbols. The most important tool? The remote control for the heating.

Welcome to Freemasonry, where the only thing stronger than our bonds of brotherhood is the smell of our lodge's antiques.

You'll find that Masonic lessons are everywhere. Even in the mystery of the missing gavel.

In Freemasonry, we value discretion. That's why we discreetly judge each other's raffle donations.

Freemasonry teaches you to be circumspect. Which is just a fancy way of saying, 'Don't trip over the altar.'

Remember, the journey of a thousand miles begins with a single step. And probably a few wrong turns in the lodge hallways.

Freemasonry: Where you're encouraged to reflect deeply on life, the universe, and where you left your ritual book.

You're about to learn the ancient art of Masonic memory work. Also known as the art of panicking quietly.

"In the lodge, we uphold the highest standards of ethics and morality. And the lowest standards for lodge wine."

> Welcome to the brotherhood. Just remember, the most profound Masonic secret is still how to get your apron size right.

Masonry teaches us to build better men. And occasionally, a halfway decent shed.

In Freemasonry, every man is your brother. Which means you now have an excuse when you forget names: 'Sorry, brother!'

You're joining a tradition that spans centuries. Including the century-old debate over who's hosting the next social night.

Remember, in Freemasonry, we aim to smooth our rough ashlars. Which is a lot harder than it sounds, especially after whisky.

Freemasonry: Where you can find ancient wisdom, moral improvement, and a surprisingly competitive BBQ cook-off.

"

In the lodge, we're all about symbols. Like the symbol of a closed wallet during subs month.

Joining Freemasonry means you're part of a global fraternity. It also means you're part of global confusion over ritual variations.

You'll find that being a Freemason is about more than just meetings. It's also about finding good excuses to miss those meetings.

As a new candidate, you'll embark on a journey of self-improvement, enlightenment, and wondering why we still use snail mail for summons.

Freemasonry is about building bridges. And occasionally, about trying to fix the lodge's actual bridge.

You'll learn the importance of the square and compass. And the even greater importance of remembering where you parked.

Freemasonry: where you'll gain profound insights into the nature of reality. And into the nature of making small talk at social events.

In the lodge, you'll find brotherhood, wisdom, and the occasional argument over which way the toilet paper roll should go.

Remember, the goal of Freemasonry is to make good men better. And to make long meetings shorter... we're still working on that one.

In Freemasonry, every man is a brother. Which means you'll finally understand why brothers always fight over the remote.

Welcome to a world of mystery, tradition, and the sacred quest to find a comfortable chair during lodge meetings.

Remember, as a Freemason, you're part of a historic brotherhood. And part of historic debates over what to order for your meal at the Ladies Festival.

Freemasonry: Where you learn to use the tools of the craft. And where you learn that the most important tool is always missing.

You'll soon understand the Masonic journey is about personal growth. And about growing your collection of Masonic ties.
Wear the wrong one and it's a £5 fine!

In Freemasonry, we aim to light the path of wisdom. Just as soon as we figure out how to replace the lightbulb in the lodge hall.

You're about to learn that Masonic secrets aren't just about ancient rituals. They're also about who drank the last glass of wine.

In the lodge, we're all about harmony and unity. Until it's time to decide on the next social event.

Freemasonry teaches the importance of balance. Like balancing your Masonic duties and your desire to nap.

You'll learn the value of Masonic symbols. And the value of a good pair of comfortable shoes for those long, standing ceremonies.

In Freemasonry, every tool has a lesson. Including the lesson of 'Please return the tools where you found them.'

You're joining a fraternity known for its secrets. Like the secret of how to look dignified in an apron.

Freemasonry: Where you'll find the keys to moral and spiritual growth. And occasionally, the keys someone left behind at the last meeting.

In the lodge, you'll learn to trust your brothers. Especially when you're trusting them not to laugh at your first attempt at ritual work.

Welcome to Freemasonry, where every meeting is an opportunity to learn, grow, and sneak in a hip flask.

You'll discover that being a Freemason means more than just attending meetings. It means also attending the pub.

In Freemasonry, we're all about building character. And about occasionally misplacing the gavel.

In Freemasonry, we're not just about square and compasses. We're also about squaring away a glass of wine during the festive board.

Joining a lodge means you'll master Masonic rituals and the fine art of queuing for the bar after the meeting.

"

A Freemason's apron is not just a symbol of his rank, but also a handy place to wipe crumbs after the festive board.

Becoming a Freemason means you're skilled in ancient rituals and navigating rain to get to your lodge meetings.

In Freemasonry, the secret handshake is less about secrecy and more about avoiding a limp fish handshake at the festive board.

" Lodges are renowned for their history, their heritage, and their heated debates over whether it's scone as in 'gone' or scone as in 'cone' and don't get us started on 'Bath' or 'Frome!' "

Joining a lodge means embracing Masonic values and the undying hope for a sunny day for the annual lodge BBQ.

The Great Architect in Freemasonry must love rain, given how often He schedules it for our outdoor events.

Remember, a true Freemason not only masters the art of the ritual but also the art of complaining about the weather with dignity.

> The Masonic journey includes enlightenment, brotherhood, and a lifelong quest for the perfect pork pie at the festive board.

Freemasonry teaches us many things. In Britain, it's that brotherly love extends to offering your mate the last biscuit.

Freemasonry: where every meeting is an opportunity for spiritual growth and a good moan about the traffic getting to lodge.

You'll soon learn that the most challenging part of Freemasonry isn't the ritual work; it's resisting the second helping of pudding.

In our lodges, we aim for
moral and spiritual elevation.
And we aim to do it before
the pub stops serving.

"

"

Becoming a Freemason means you've joined a fraternity with centuries of history. And centuries of jokes about how early is too early for a gin and tonic at the festive board.

"

"

Explaining balloting as a Freemason: It's like explaining gravity to a cat scared of cucumbers. 'So, one black ball can nix the whole thing?' 'Yep, and it's equally baffling.'

"

Happiness in Freemasonry is pretending the absentee on your table at the Festive Board is actually present, double dessert!

I told a new brother that addressing the Worshipful Master and then the visitors is like making tea: Worshipful Master first, as the tea, and visitors as the milk. He got so confused, now he greets everyone with 'Would you like a biscuit?'

They say the early bird catches the worm, but in our lodge, the latecomer catches Tyler's sword. It's not quite as catchy, but it definitely makes for a quicker entrance!

"

Our Tyler's sword is mostly for show, but show up late to the meeting and you'll get a performance worthy of Shakespeare. 'To be early, or not to be early, that is the question.'

"

I asked our Tyler if his sword was real. He said, 'Only if you're late.' Now I treat lodge start times like I'm defusing a bomb - precision is key!

In our lodge, the Tyler with a sword has a better track record of punctuality than Big Ben. Tick tock, brethren, lest you dance the sword ballet!

"

Being greeted by the Tyler's
sword when you're late is our
lodge's version of an
incentive program. Nothing
says 'Welcome, but you're in
trouble' like cold steel and a
disappointed frown.

"

And now, as we close the covers of this book, just like closing the Lodge.

May our bonds of brotherly love and laughter remain as steadfast as our Lodge's oldest member's claim to his favourite seat.

Until we open again, brethren, keep the Masonic light in your hearts and a good joke on your lips.

S.M.I.B